CW01183804

JUNIOR SURVIVAL LIBRARY

The World's Tallest Animal Story

THE GIRAFFE

Jeremy Bradshaw

ANGLIA
Television Limited

Boxtree

Key to abbreviations

lb	pound
gm	gramme
kg	kilogram
in	inch
ft	foot
yd	yard
cm	centimetre
m	metre
km	kilometre
sq mile	square mile
sq km	square kilometre
kph	kilometres per hour
mph	miles per hour

First published in 1990 by Boxtree Limited
Copyright © 1990 Survival Anglia Limited
Text copyright © 1990 Jeremy Bradshaw

Front jacket photograph: Jen and Des Bartlett
Survival Anglia
(Giraffe and springbuck)
Back jacket photograph:
Survival Anglia/Alan Root
(Giraffes at sunset in the Serengeti)

British Library Cataloguing in Publication Data
Bradshaw, Jeremy
  The giraffe.
  1. Giraffes.
  I. Title II. Series
  599.7357

ISBN 1-85283-068-9

Edited by Miranda Smith
Designed by Groom & Pickerill
Typeset by Rowland Phototypesetting Limited
Bury St Edmunds, Suffolk

Printed and bound in Italy
by OFSA s.p.a.

for Boxtree Limited,
36 Tavistock Street,
London WC2E 7PB

Contents

The 'camelopard' 4

Giant of the savannah 6

Type of giraffe 8

Hooves and horns 10

Moving about 12

A life in the day 14

Thorny delights 16

Drinking 18

Animals that browse 20

Enemies 22

First days of life 24

The nursery 26

Saved from extinction? 28

Glossary 30

Index 31

Acknowledgements
and Notes on author 32

The 'camelopard'

In 1826, a strange 13-foot-high animal arrived by ship at the port of Marseille in southern France. It was said to be a 'camelopard' – a cross between a camel and a leopard. Accompanied by a police escort, it was then walked 800 kms (500 miles) to Paris, where more than 10,000 people came to see it. They were told that this animal was not a mythical beast come to life, nor a giant form of a species. It was a young giraffe, a gift from the ruler of Egypt to the king of France.

This was the first time that most Europeans had seen a giraffe. When Samuel Johnson set eyes on a drawing of a giraffe half a century before, he did not know how to describe it. The best he could come up with was 'taller than an elephant but not so thick'. In many ways the slender giraffe is still a puzzling animal today. It looks as if it has been put together from parts of other animals. The face, particularly the lips, is rather like a camel's, though the horns do not seem quite right. The coat can have blotchy spots rather like a leopard's, although sometimes it looks more like crazy paving. The hooves are like a cow's. In fact, it was once thought that the giraffe was a cross between a hyena, a camel and a cow.

The word 'giraffe' may well come from the Arabic word *xirapha* meaning 'the one who moves quickly'. The highest recommendation that an Arab can give a horse is to say that it can overtake a giraffe.

Today, it is known that the giraffe is a **species** in its own right. And some remarkable facts about the way of life of this often surprising creature have come to light in the last few years. A giraffe seen in a zoo is not the same as a giraffe in its natural **habitat** on the wide plains of the **savannah**. Amongst the flat-topped thorn trees it is one of the most serene and graceful animals on earth. And there can be no more beautiful sight than a group of giraffes slowly crossing the plains of Africa. At a distance they look like masted ships sailing over a sea of grass.

Right *The giraffe's coat can look like crazy paving.*

Left *One of the first giraffes to be seen in Europe is led by its Egyptian keepers.*

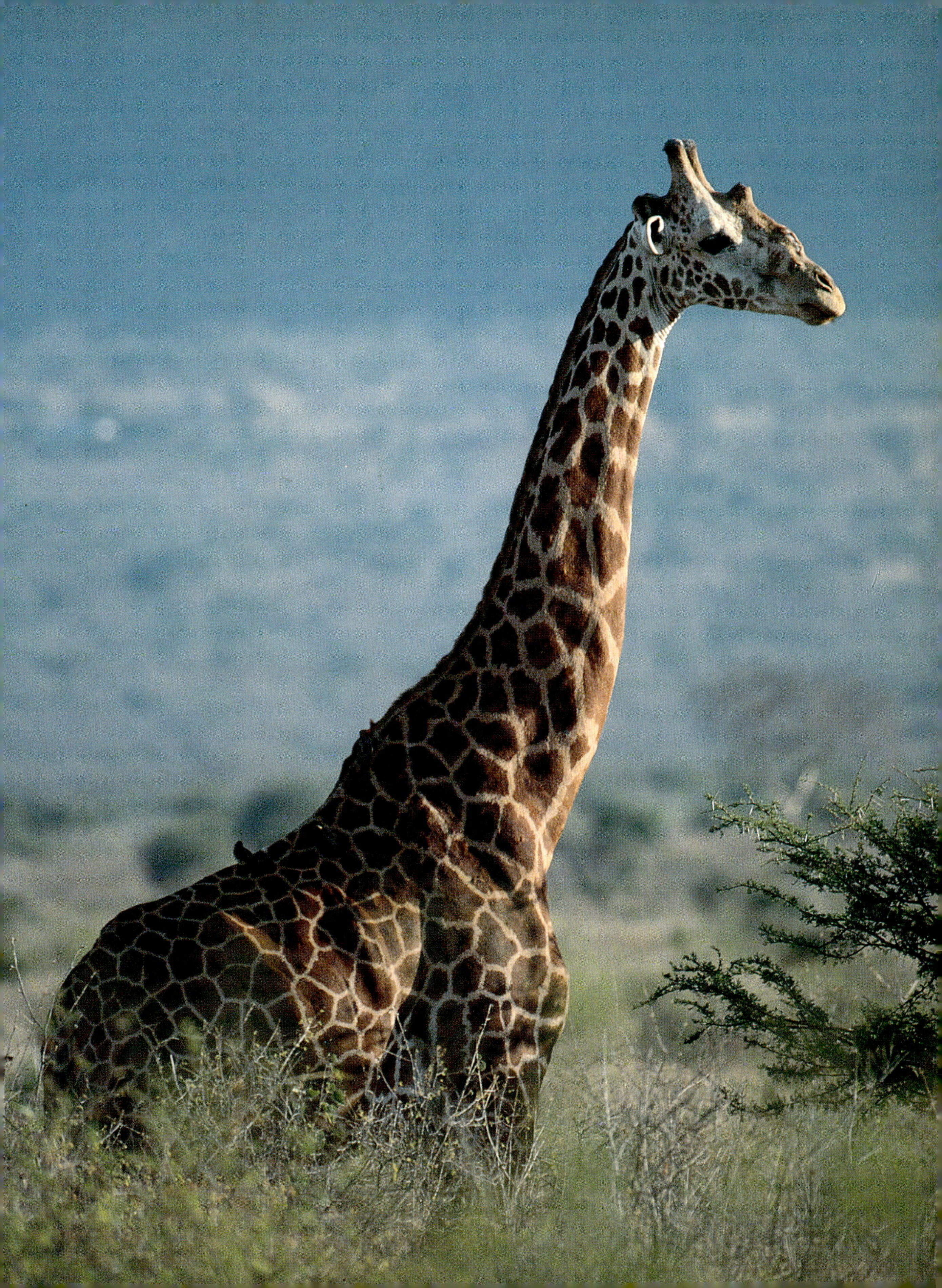

Giant of the savannah

The question often asked about giraffes is: how did they ever get to be so tall? No other animal alive today comes anywhere near them in terms of height.

The answer would seem to be that the giraffe is the sole survivor of a race of giants. Millions of years ago, there were many tall animals on the African savannah, all browsing on the trees. There were large animals with weird-sounding names like sivatheres, baluchitheres, mastodonts and deinotheres, whose **fossilised** bones have been discovered. Some of these animals were tall, so the giraffes had to become taller, through the process of **evolution**, in order to compete. But then, for some reason, the other creatures died out, leaving the giraffe towering above the earth.

Left *A Cape giraffe towers over zebra at a waterhole in Etosha National Park, South West Africa.*

Below *A Sivatherium – an ancient type of giraffe with antlers – browses behind some primitive men.*

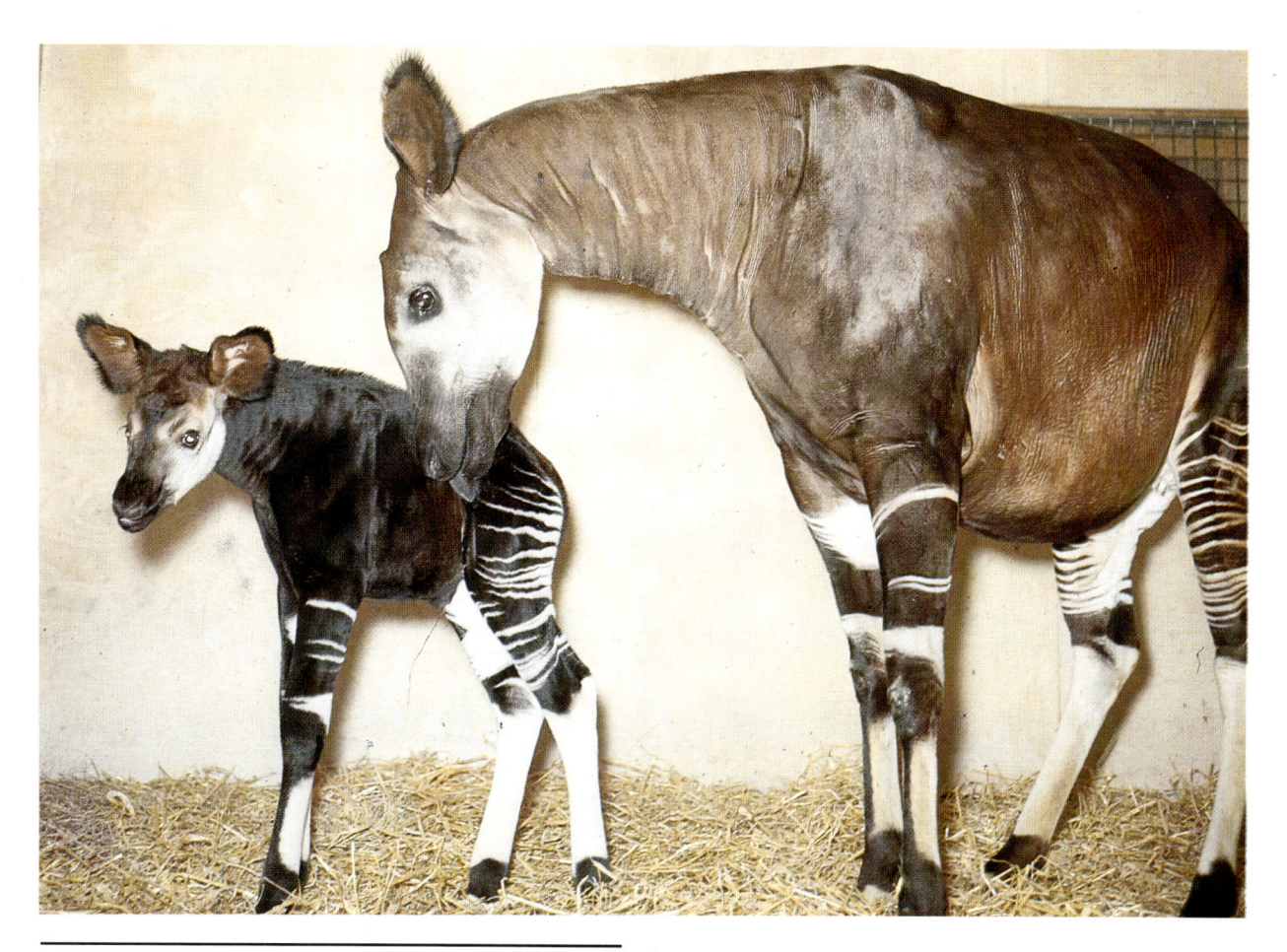

A mother okapi and her youngster at Bristol Zoo.

A bull giraffe can measure up to 5 m (16 ft) in height. That lofty position allows it to reach up as high as any other land living animal except the elephant (but that's only because it has a trunk to help it). When bull giraffes meet, they establish by various signals which is superior. Master bulls carry their heads higher, with their chins tilted up. If a smaller male is feeding in a tree, and a more powerful bull comes along, then the smaller one will probably walk away and find its food elsewhere.

One of the remarkable things about a giraffe's neck is how few bones it contains. It has just seven, which is exactly the same as all other mammals, including ourselves. During the process of evolution, each bone – or vertebra – in the giraffe's neck has extended. But the number has stayed the same. Our neck bones are less than an inch long, on average, while the giraffe's are 15 times longer – or one foot in length.

The okapi

The okapi is the giraffe's only living relative and was once equally mysterious. It was one of the last big mammals to be discovered in Africa and is now very rare, living deep in the rainforests of Central Africa.

The okapi's neck is extremely **flexible**, although it is not as long as a giraffe's. However the general body shape of the two animals is the same. The adult okapi stands almost 2 m (6½ ft) high, less than half the height of a giraffe. It eats leaves and grass, and has a long mobile tongue like the giraffe's.

Type of giraffe

Many of the tallest giraffes in the world come from Kenya and Tanzania. These are called Masai giraffes after the cattle-herding tribe that inhabits large areas of east Africa.

There is one basic model of giraffe, but it comes in several different finishes. The main characteristics that differ are the colour of the coat and the number of the horns. There are eight **subspecies**: the Nubian, the Reticulated, the Masai, Rothschild's Giraffe, the West African, the Angolan, the Cape Giraffe and Thornicroft's Giraffe. Many of these look rather similar, but one stands out – the Reticulated. Its coat is more distinctive than the others and looks like crazy paving.

Below *The Nubian Giraffe, which occurs in the Sudan, has softer, less defined markings.*

Left *Thornicroft's giraffe live in the Luangwa River valley in Zambia.*

8

The Reticulated Giraffe lives in the dry country of Kenya, Somali and southern Ethiopia. Some say it is the most beautiful sub-species of them all.

The Reticulated Giraffe lives in the dry thorn tree country of East Africa. It is the most striking of all the giraffes and shares part of its range with the colourful Samburu people. They do not harm it as the giraffes do not compete with the Samburu cattle. The giraffes like to eat the prickly leaves of the acacia thorn trees. Luckily for them, neither man nor his domestic animals has yet taken a liking to acacia thorns!

Male and female

Male giraffes are larger than the females, averaging 5 m (16 ft) and weigh about 1,400 kgs. The females are around 4.3 m (14 ft) in height and weigh around 800 kgs.

The males are distinguished not only by their larger size but also by their horns which often have shiny tops. The horns are thicker and more prominent, and are often hairless because the males hit them against rivals when they fight, rubbing away the hair. By contrast, the female's horns are more slender.

Hooves and horns

Different groups of animals have different types of feet. Some have claws like cats and dogs. Those with hooves are called **ungulates**, and the giraffe is an ungulate. There are two types of ungulate – odd and even-toed. Odd-toed ungulates include horses, rhinoceroses and tapirs. Even-toed ungulates are animals like cows, antelopes, deer, hippopotamuses, pigs – and the giraffe.

Although scientists like to put similar animals into tidy groups, or **genuses**, the giraffe has defeated them. The animal has cloven hooves that look rather like those of a giant cow, so originally it was grouped with them. But other things, for example its horns, suggest that the giraffe is more like a deer than a cow. However, deer shed their horns every year and grow new ones. Giraffes do not do this. And so the giraffe was put back in the genus that contained cows. But then it was noticed that cows have horny horns and giraffes have hairy horns. Confused? Well, so were the scientists, and they finally decided that giraffes were so odd that they had better have a genus of their own.

Many male hooved animals have horns and they use them to fight with when it comes to the mating season. Horns may be sharp and pointed, like an antelope's, or branched like those of a deer. The males lock or clash horns in a battle to establish which is stronger. The more powerful males will win more mates.

Male giraffes fight too, but their horns are small for their body size and less important in combat. It is male giraffes that are around the same size that come into conflict. They hurl their heads and horns at each other, landing sledgehammer blows on the neck, body and legs of their opponent. Despite the vigour of these attacks, the bulls seldom seriously hurt one another.

To cushion the impact as a giraffe's head crashes into the side of its opponent, the skull is strengthened with layers of bone which act like a kind of crash helmet. The skin is also exceptionally tough.

Left *The hippopotamus has four toes and is an even-toed ungulate like the giraffe.*

Opposite *A male giraffe in a sea of flowers brought on by the annual rain.*

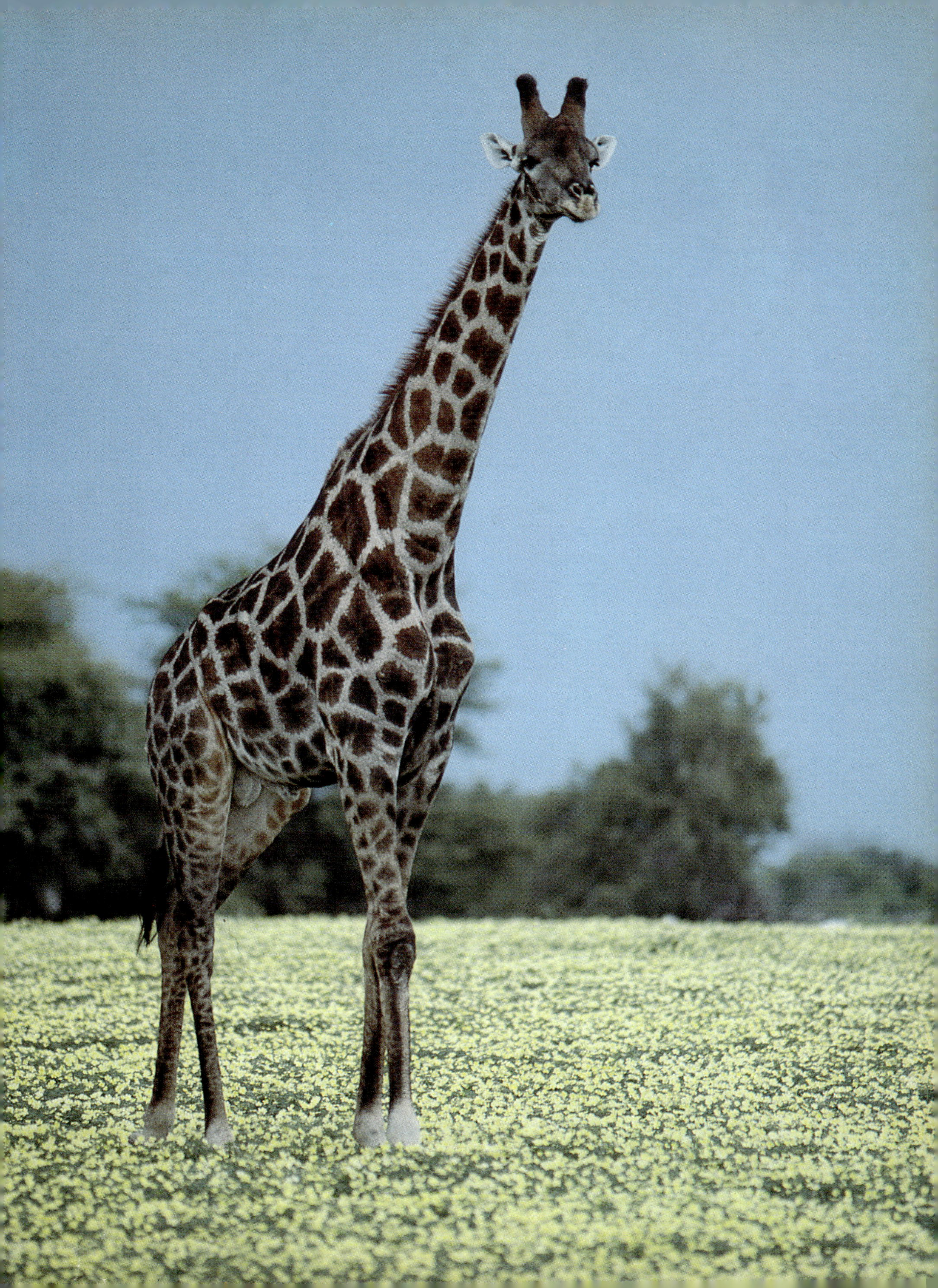

Moving about

Giraffes are bulky and lanky. Moving around, a giraffe experiences unique difficulties.

Of all the land mammals, the giraffe probably has the greatest problem getting up from the ground after resting. It takes about four seconds for it to organise its legs alone, First it throws its neck forward to give it the **momentum** necessary to lift the hind legs. It is the same principle used when you throw yourself forward to get out of a chair. After a two second pause, the giraffe rocks backwards to get its front legs up. Then it is ready to walk.

A closer examination of a walking giraffe reveals that the neck moves backwards and forwards twice during each stride. Because the legs are so long, they do not move like the legs of other large animals. Most large animals move diagonally opposite legs together – their front left and back right, or front right and back left. You can see this best if you watch a horse trotting. The giraffe moves both right legs together and then both left legs together. If they did not move both legs on the same side together, the legs would probably crash into each other.

A giraffe crosses a kopje, or rocky outcrop, in the Serengeti in Tanzania.

A group of giraffe gallops across the savannah grassland. They can outrun most predators.

Moving in this way, a giraffe cannot manoeuvre easily. It cannot stop quickly, or start quickly, or turn on a sixpence. But then it is seldom surprised on the open plains it inhabits, and in any case it has few enemies.

A giraffe cannot trot because of the length of its legs. It simply breaks into a gallop. The front legs move together, and the hind legs **straddle** the forelegs. A giraffe can gallop for hours without tiring. As it speeds away it can often throw up loose stones and clods of earth. In fact, it was once thought that the giraffe purposely pelted any pursuer with stones.

Built for speed?

No two people agree on whether a giraffe is ugly or graceful when it moves fast. The neck seems to work overtime, and to be out of rhythm with the legs, giving a jerky movement. One problem with long legs is that their long muscles **contract** relatively slowly, so the gallop may only reach 56 kph (35 mph), which may not seem very fast for such long legs. However, this speed is usually quite enough to get the animal out of trouble. Giraffes can jump as well, and have been seen to negotiate a 1.5 metre (4½ ft) high fence!

A life in the day

A herd of deer or a flock of birds look as though they are a unit. The individuals react together and react to each other. However, a group of giraffes do no such thing. They are like a group of people who never talk to one another but who stay vaguely in each other's company.

A herd of giraffes, containing perhaps twelve individuals, might be spread over 1.6 kms (1 mile). There is no doubt that they can see each other – giraffes have much better eyesight than humans – but they seldom communicate. The only way that it can be seen that they are a herd is that, over a period of time, the animals will move in the same direction. There are no leaders and the individuals in the group may change from day to day.

Why giraffes live in herds is a mystery. It has been suggested that they do it because of

Chewing the cud

While a giraffe rests, it chews the cud. This involves **regurgitating** leaves from the stomach, chewing them thoroughly and then swallowing them again. If you watch a giraffe's neck closely you can see the tennis-ball-sized pieces of food going up and down. Chewing the cud allows an animal to feed fast, and then to chew it over later on. Vegetable matter often needs a lot of chewing to get all the goodness out of it.

Giraffe's 'watchtower' vision allows them to keep their companions in view over great distances.

Their large appetites mean that giraffes may need to browse during the night.

predators – many pairs of eyes watching for danger is better than one. However, there is little evidence for this. If one giraffe snorts in alarm at a lion and runs off, the chances are that the other giraffes will take no notice. Interestingly, other animals, like zebra, often stay near giraffes because the giraffes will give them early warning of danger from their 'watchtowers'.

It may be that giraffes simply group together because their food trees grow in a particular place. Or maybe they simply like the undemanding company of others of their species.

A giraffe's daily routine is measured and unhurried. It spends most hours of the day feeding. It starts when the sun rises, and **browses** until midday. Then it will stop and rest for an hour or so. It does not have to seek shade, although the sun burns down on it, because it can lose heat through its neck and legs.

In the afternoon, the giraffe will start feeding again. It does so until sundown when it is time to look for a place to sleep. However, it may continue to feed for a while after dark. At 11 pm, it may lie down for two to four hours. It might even sleep for half an hour, but it never goes into a deep sleep for more than two minutes at any one time.

Thorny delights

Giraffes spend more than two-thirds of their lives feeding – on average more than sixteen hours a day. That is 33.7 kgs (75 lbs) of food. Giraffes eat so much that they can change the shape of the trees that they browse on.

Giraffes feed primarily on trees and shrubs. The leaves of acacia trees form one of the most important parts of their diet, but creepers, vines, bark, fruits and grass also feature on their menu. Acacias come in many shapes and sizes and most of them are covered in long spines. It is interesting that in Australia, where there are no giraffes, the acacias do not have thorns.

On the plains of Africa, there are 'wait-a-bit' thorn bushes, whistling thorns and the yellow-barked acacia or fever trees. You would know if you walked into a wait-a-bit thorn bush because it would make you wait – probably for at least ten minutes while you extracted the spines.

Whistling thorns grow up to 3 m (9½ft) in height, but in areas where giraffes are common, the browsing keeps them down to bushes of 2 m (6 ft) high.

When the acacia trees flower in Namibia, the Cape giraffe are quick to move in.

The giraffe's mouth

A large bull giraffe can extend its normal reach by as much as 45 cms (18 ins). It does so by reaching out its enormously long tongue, and using it almost like a lassoo, curling it around a branch and bringing it down within reach of its mouth. The fruits of the sausage tree (so called because the fruit is shaped like a big sausage on a string) are lassooed in the same way.

When an antelope feeds, it grasps the twig or leaf in its mouth and snips it off. However, a giraffe will grip a branch between its jaws and comb off the leaves and twigs with its lower front teeth, leaving the woody bits behind. Its lips appear to be relatively thornproof; in fact the giraffe often eats the softer thorns.

Right *Using its tongue, a giraffe can reach leaves up to eighteen and a half feet above the ground.*

Below *Giraffes naturally practise the art of tree-shaping, or topiary.*

Out on the drier savannah, the acacias look as if someone has removed all the branches and leaves below 5 m (16 ft) with a pair of shears. The trunk looks like a stalk. This is simply because the giraffe eats everything **palatable** it can reach up to that height, making what is known as a 'browse line'.

Giraffes do occasionally fall when they are feeding at full stretch. One animal was found with its head caught in the fork of a tree. It had been feeding on a slope and its legs had slipped from under it. Fortunately, it was possible to raise the animal back onto its feet with the help of a winch.

Drinking

In a zoo, a giraffe may drink as much as 50 litres (11 gallons) of water a day. However, in the wild a giraffe may go a whole week without a drink. This is because there is water in the acacia leaves that form such a large part of its diet. An acacia leaf, like the human body, may be two-thirds water.

From time to time, especially during the African dry season, a giraffe will venture to a **waterhole** or river for a drink. A giraffe in search of a drink is often nervous. Predators may be lurking near water sources. A lion will grab a giraffe by the head or neck if it can

Right *Predators often lurk near waterholes, so drinking in groups is safer.*

A rush of blood to the head

A giraffe has very high blood pressure, and when the head is lowered to drink, the whole of the body's blood is being forced into it by **gravity**. For many years, it was not understood why this blood pressure did not burst the giraffe's brain when it bent down to drink. Now it is known that the giraffe has a wonderful network of spongey blood vessels near the brain that absorb the initial surge of blood to the brain. It also has a unique system of **valves** which prevent the pressure building up.

While drinking, the giraffe has to adopt a very awkward looking position.

reach, and a crocodile would seize a giraffe whose nose was too close to the water.

When a giraffe is reasonably sure that there is no predator nearby at a watering place, it will **splay** its front legs in a series of jerky movements. It then lowers its head slowly.

When the giraffe has drunk its fill, usually in a few minutes, it raises its head again and jerks its legs back together. As anyone who has got up from lying on the floor will know, if this is done too quickly it can cause you to feel faint. The giraffe has the same problem, so it has to raise its head carefully.

Animals that browse

There are two types of ungulate on the African savannah: grazers and browsers. Grazing animals like zebra and wildebeest eat grass. Browsing animals, like giraffes, eat parts of trees and shrubs. Browsing animals can live together in the same woodlands without fighting over food because they eat different plants at different levels. But the giraffe still has some competition – from elephants, from rhino and from some antelope.

Lit by the early morning light, this giraffe will soon be browsing trees nearby on the savannah.

At the lower levels, the impala antelope will, if grass runs short, eat the same shoots as the giraffe. But impala can reach only four or five feet high. An eland, however, which is often six feet at the shoulder, can reach some of the food the giraffe likes. For example, it nibbles at the yellow acacia blossoms.

Black rhinos relish acacia thorns so tough and sharp that they could puncture the tyres of a jeep. Giraffes baulk at such food because the skin on the inside of their mouths and on their tongues is not as leathery as that of the rhinos. Their teeth are not as strong either. But the

Left *With its trunk at full stretch, an elephant can reach higher than a giraffe.*

The gerenuk

This East African antelope has found a similar solution to the problem of reaching leaves on trees. Its long neck lets it reach higher than any other antelope. It can also stand on two legs. Like the giraffe, it has long mobile lips. It selects only the juiciest shoots on the trees, getting most of its water this way.

Below *A gerenuk is the only antelope that can manoevre while standing on two legs.*

giraffe can still eat the tender shoots at the top, several metres above the rhino's reach.

Only one animal can reach higher from the ground than a giraffe: the elephant. While the two are not serious competitors for food, they do have an effect upon one another. In places where elephants outstrip their food supply, they rob the giraffe of theirs.

In the past, elephants have devastated great areas of giraffe country in East Africa. The elephants had been driven out of areas occupied by man, and forced into areas without enough food to support them. In Tsavo National Park, for example, elephants pushed over and killed many thousands of acacia trees to eat the leaves and bark.

Because giraffe are adaptable, they have survived by feeding on smaller trees and bushes that the elephants left behind. But in some places, the combined effect of giraffes and elephants has turned the savannah woodlands into thick scrub. The trees are stunted because the giraffe trim them before they have a chance to grow.

Enemies

One of the great advantages of large size to an animal is that it is heavy and powerful. Consequently, it has few enemies. This is true for the elephant, the rhinoceros and the buffalo. By and large, the giraffe is not often attacked by predators. However, there is one exception – the lion.

A pride of lions compete over the carcass of a young giraffe that they killed thirty minutes before.

Lions do not choose giraffes as **prey** animals very often. One reason is that giraffes are very wary. With their watchtower vision, they can spot a lion or a **pride** of lions two miles (three kms) away. Giraffes are particularly good at detecting movement, but can also see colours, and will spot a sandy-coloured lion if it is not **camouflaged**. Once a lion knows it is being watched, it will seldom try to hunt the watcher.

Whether a giraffe can **scent** a lion is not known. Sense of smell does not seem to be as important to a giraffe as sight. But they most certainly can smell. At London Zoo, several giraffes once refused to eat food prepared by a man who had previously handled mice. The smell obviously put them off!

Leopards are much smaller than lions – only half the size – and hunting a giraffe would simply not cross their minds. However, in one unfortunate incident, a male giraffe was browsing in a tree unaware that a leopard was asleep on one of the branches. The leopard suddenly woke and probably thought that a large animal was about to attack it so it launched itself ferociously at the giraffe's neck. The giraffe died, but the leopard apparently made no attempt to eat it.

This lioness will almost certainly be outpaced by the giraffes and give up her hunt.

Lions, on the other hand, do occasionally try to hunt giraffes, especially the males that are more likely to be alone, and hence easier to creep up on. But the lion must be very careful. One kick from those long legs can smash a lion's skull; a giraffe once kicked the passenger door right off a safari bus!

Giraffes are in a strong position to defend themselves and in many cases lions will withdraw to try their luck on less dangerous prey. Giraffe calves *are* more at risk from lions. But their mothers can successfully defend them with their flailing hooves. However, the calf will sometimes get in the way, and may be unlucky enough to get hurt by its own mother.

First days of life

A giraffe's first experience is being dropped 2 m (6½ ft) onto its head. This is because a mother giraffe gives birth in a standing position.

When a female giraffe is about to go into **labour**, she leaves the other females of her group and goes to a place where she will be hidden by trees. She may be accompanied by a female 'companion'. Why another female is present at the birth is not known. It may be to help defend the calf should a lion turn up, or it may be that it will be a useful experience when the companion has a calf of her own.

Once the baby has landed on the ground, it must try to get to its feet as quickly as possible. There are two reasons for this. Firstly, it is very **vulnerable** if it cannot run. Hyenas, lions or even cheetahs might dash in. Secondly, a young giraffe needs to stand up to be able to reach its mother's **teats**.

Usually within an hour of birth, the ungainly youngster is finding its feet. It is 1.8 metres (6 ft) in height and 67.5 kgs (150 lbs) in weight. It takes the mother time to get used to the idea that she has a youngster, but as it **suckles** and she licks it, a **bond** is established.

Though still rather wobbly, the calf will soon gather strength by feeding on its

A mother's tongue

It has been said that the mother giraffe's tongue is so rough that a calf hides for the first four days to avoid it. This is just one of the many 'tall' stories about the giraffe! In fact, the mother uses her tongue quite delicately. Licking the calf clean as it suckles helps her to learn her calf's scent.

A mother nuzzles her hour-old calf. It is six feet tall and can already walk.

mother's milk. At this stage, the milk is five times richer in protein than cow's milk, and on this highly **nutritious** diet, the youngster may grow as much as 15 cms (6 ins) a day!

If the calf feels threatened, it will take refuge under its mother's belly. This is the position in which she can best defend it. The mother and her calf will join up with other females after three or four days. If there are several calves about, the first thing they do is touch nostrils. Then the pair will put their heads to the ground and spring apart. This is the way young giraffes play with each other.

A mother giraffe and her calf set out to find other youngsters and form a nursery group.

The nursery

In its first year, a young giraffe grows around 2.3 metres (4 ft) in height. Half of that time will be spent away from its mother because she goes off to feed during the day. But the young calf will not be alone. It will be left in a sort of day nursery with other youngsters ranging in age from two weeks to four months.

When the adults depart in the mornings, the calves play for a while, often running together, but almost always returning to the same spot. With their tufty horns, they are the most charming babies at this stage.

The value of the day nursery is that the young do not waste energy trailing around with their parents. The calves still rely on their mother's milk. Though they nibble on acacia, they cannot yet digest it efficiently. As cud-chewers, giraffes depend on **intestinal micro-organisms** to **digest** their food. But it is not until they are four months old that the system becomes fully operational.

As the heat builds up on the savannah, some of the calves begin their afternoon **siesta**. Being under the full blaze of the midday sun does not bother a giraffe. Elephants and rhinoceroses seek shade under similar conditions, but the large surface area of a giraffe's neck and legs enables it to lose heat more efficiently.

Although the acacia scrub hides them a bit, it is surprising that more calves are not attacked by lions. A good many calves *are* killed by lions, but seldom in the nursery situation. The reason for this is that lions do not hunt when it is hot unless they have to.

By late afternoon the calves are restless and hungry. Finally, the mothers come to collect their offspring, but even now it takes a while for them to find their calves. It may be that they recognise them by smell, and it takes time because this is their weak sense. Eventually, the mothers and calves will get together, and then a suckling session takes place.

A young giraffe is suckled for five to six months. By nine months, they are fairly independent. Then it takes a further five years for them to reach full height.

Left *Lions prefer to sleep rather than hunt in the mid-day sun, so calves are safer at this time of day.*

Opposite *A Reticulated Giraffe and calf among wet season flowers of East Africa.*

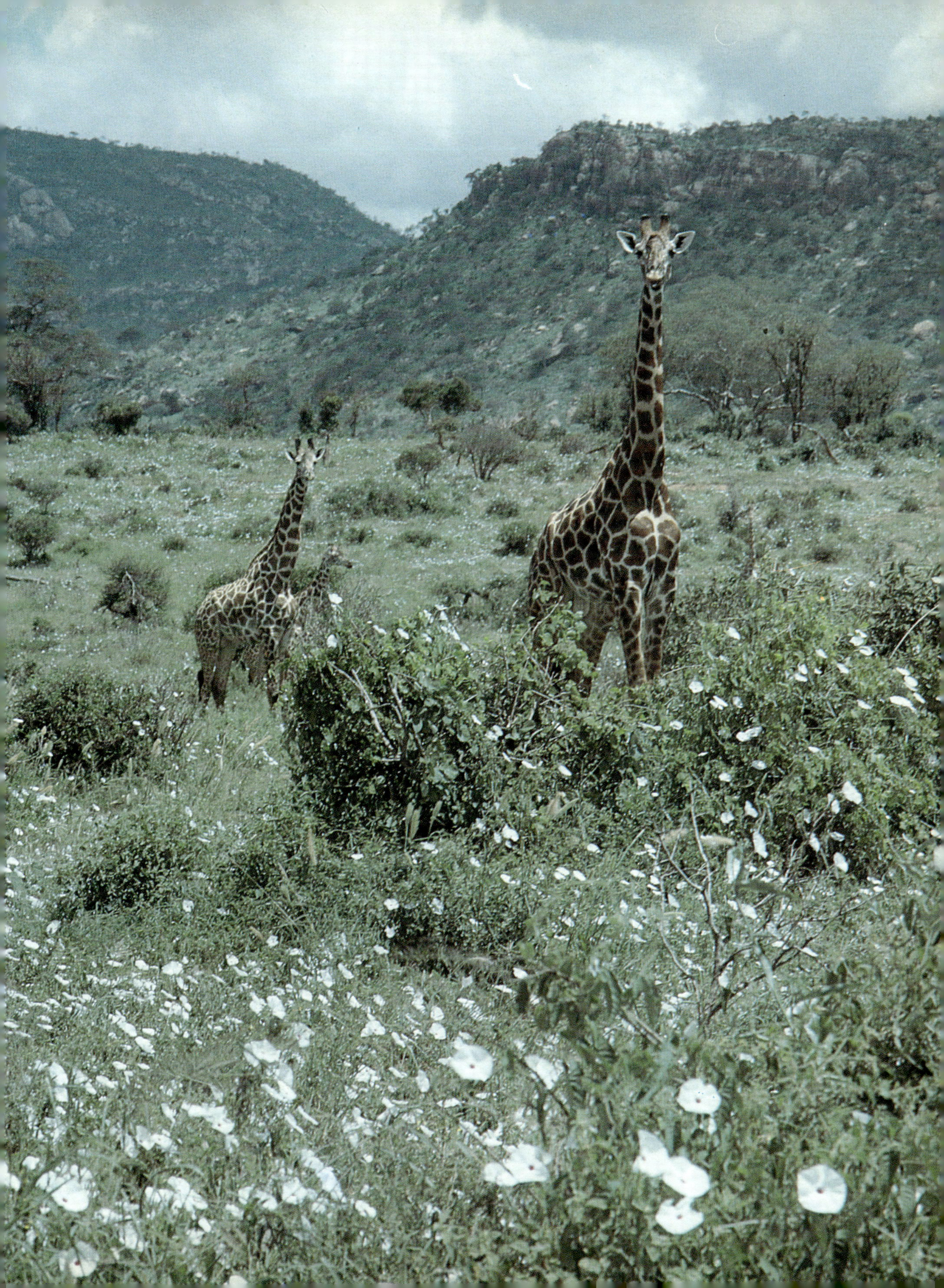

Saved from extinction?

At the end of the last century, the giraffe almost died out in southern Africa. European settlers, hunters and explorers slaughtered any giraffes they came across. This was often just to cut a strip of skin from the giraffe's lip the heel of its hind leg to make into a 6 m (19 ft) bullwhip – an indefensible act of destruction.

This hunting has now been stopped, but it wiped out the giraffe in part of its range in Southern Africa. Elsewhere, the giraffe has declined. Once, they were found right across equatorial Africa from the Atlantic Coast of

Above *The leaping dance of Samburu warriors in traditional colours in Northern Kenya.*

Right *The conservation of thorn trees is vital to the giraffe's survival.*

Senegal to the Indian ocean on the eastern seaboard. But now man's hunting and cutting down of trees has reduced their range. East Africa is the best place to see giraffes. Here, the giraffe is a protected species, and doing well.

In general, these peaceful animals do not come into conflict with man because they do not regard the foot he eats or grows as palatable. They can happily coexist with the cattle of **nomadic** tribes like the Samburu and Masai of Kenya. However, the size of the animals does sometimes cause difficulties in places closer to towns.

The problem is that a giraffe may not even notice if it walks through an electric fence or telephone wires; its hide is thick and its legs are immensely strong. The damage they do is minor, but giraffes are increasingly being confined to certain areas. As the population of Africa increases, more and more land is required for growing crops and few wild animals can be tolerated in these places.

The crucial issue for the giraffe is whether the woodlands will be preserved. As long as the trees and bushes are not felled for timber or charcoal, or to make way for agriculture, the giraffe will continue to survive. Africa's tallest animal story will also continue to be told for many years to come.

Due to hunting, the population of giraffes in Southern Africa was very low. Now their future looks more secure.

Glossary

Bond A closeness formed between mother and offspring

Browse To feed on leaves, young shoots and other vegetation

Camouflage The ability to hide by appearing to be part of the natural background

Contract To become reduced in size by being drawn together

Digest To break down substances and absorb them

Evolution The process by which creatures and plants have slowly developed and changed over many thousands or millions of years

Flexible That which will bend

Fossil A skeleton, footprint or leaf imprint from the past embedded in the earth's crust

Genus A class or group that share the same characteristics

Gravity

Habitat The environment in which an animal usually lives

Intestinal micro-organisms Bacteria that live inside the digestive system of a creature

Labour The process of giving birth

Momentum The force gained through movement

Nomadic Leading a wandering life, with no fixed home

Nutritious Nourishing, aiding growth and development

Palatable Tasting nice enough to eat

Predator An animal that lives by hunting other animals

Prey An animal that is eaten by a predator

Pride A group or family of lions

Regurgitate To bring up partially digested food

Savannah Open grassland of the tropical and subtropical regions

Scent To identify by means of the sense of smell

Siesta A short sleep or rest

Species A kind, variety or type of animal

Splay To spread out the legs

Straddle To spread wide apart, astride or on either side

Subspecies A subdivision of a species, usually because of geographical location

Suckle To take milk from the teats of the mother giraffe

Teats The mammary glands of a mammal

Ungulate Mammal with hooves

Valve A structure in the arteries or veins of an animal that controls the flow of blood

Vulnerable Unprotected from danger

Waterhole A pool used by animals for drinking and bathing

Index

The entries in **bold** are illustrations.

Africa 4, 6, **6**, 7, 16, 17, 20, 21, 26, **27**, 28, 29
   Ethiopia 9
   Kenya 8, 9
   Namibia **16**
   Senegal 29
   Somali 9
   Sudan 8
   Tanzania 8, **12**
   Zambia 8
antelopes 17, 20
   eland 20
   impala 20

birth 24
blood pressure 18
bonding 24, 30
buffalo 22
bullwhip 28

calves 23, **24**, 24–5, **25**, 26 26–7
camelopard 4–5
camouflage 22, 30
coat 4, 8
communication 7
competition 20
   antelope 20
   elephants 20
   rhino 20–1
cows 10

deer 10, 14
defence 23, 25
drinking 18–19

elephants 7, **21**, 21–2
endangered species 28
explorers 28
eyesight (watchtower vision) 14, **14**, 15, 22

fighting, 9, 10
food 7, 9, 14–15, 16–17, 26
   browsing 15, 16, 17, 20–1, 30
   chewing the cud 14, 26
   grazing 20
   sausage trees 17
   thorn trees 9, 16–17, **17**, 18, 20, 26
fossils 6, 30

gerenuk 21, **21**
giraffe
   Angolan 8
   Cape **6**, 8
   cheetahs and 24
   early species 6
   getting up 12
   hyenas and 24
   lions and 24
   Masai 8
   Nubian 8, **8**
   origin of name 4
   Reticulated 8, **9**, **26**
   Rothschild's 8
   size 6, 7, 8, 9, 26, 29
   Thornicroft's 8, **8**
   West African 8

habitat 4, 6, 17, 20, 26, 30
herding 14–15
hippopotamus 10
hooves 4, 10–11
horns 9, 10–11
horse 4, 12
hunting 28, **29**

Johnson, Samuel 4

legs 12, 13, 15, 19, 23
leopard 4, 23
lips 4

Masai, the 29
movement 12–13, **13**

necks 7, 12, 13, 15
nurseries 25, 26–7

okapi 7, **7**
   food 7
   size 7
   tongues 7

predators 13, 15 18, 30
   crocodiles 19
   lions 15, 18–19, 22, **22**, **23**, 26

rainforests 7
rhinoceros 22

Samburu, the 9, 29
scenting 23, 26
siesta 26, 30
Sivatherium 6, **6**
sleep 15
suckling 26, 30

teeth 17, 20
tongues 7, 17, **17**, **18**, 20, 24
Tsavo National Park 21

ungulates 10, 20, 30

waterholes 18, 30
wildebeest 20

zebra **6**, 15, 20
zoos 4, 18
   Bristol **7**
   London 23

31

Picture Acknowledgements

The publishers would like to thank the
Survival Anglia picture library
and the following photographers for the use
of photographs on the pages listed:

Bruce Davidson 5, 17 (right), 26, 28 (right); Lee Lyon 6 (top); Maurice Tibbles 7; Cindy Buxton 8 (left); J. P. Bradshaw 8 (right); Alan Root 9, 12, 21 (bottom), 27; Bob Campbell 10, 20, 24; Jen and Des Bartlett 11, 15, 16, 18, 19, 22, 23, 29; Richard and Julia Kemp 13; Jeff Foott 17 (left), 25, 28 (left); J. B. Davidson 14.

About the author

Jeremy Bradshaw grew up in the Sussex Weald. He studied Zoology at Oxford University, and has made more than a hundred natural history and environmental programmes for Survival Anglia where he is senior producer. He travelled to East Africa to film giraffes, and his previous publications include a book on Animal Giants.

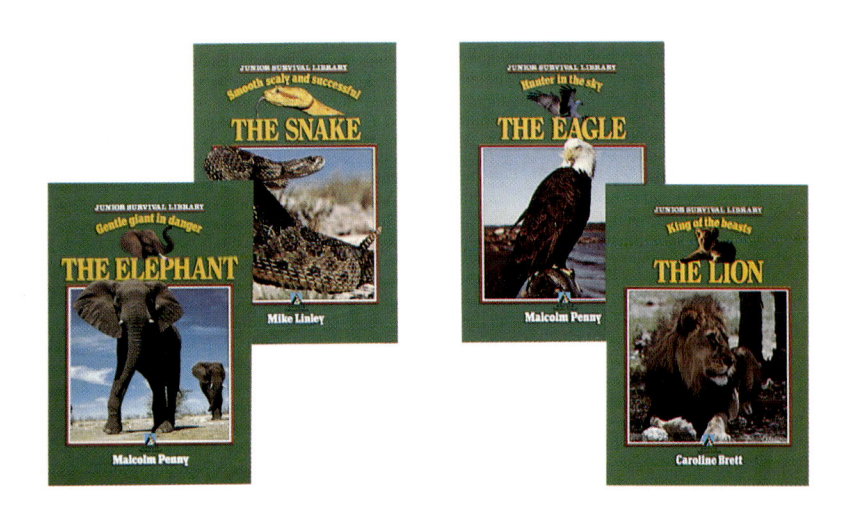

The first four titles in the Junior Survival Library.